Poems Throughout the Year and Beyond by Linda Taylor
Copyright ©2001, 2019 Linda Taylor

All rights reserved. No part of this book may be reproduced or transmitted in any form or by any means, electronic or mechanical, including photocopying, recording, or by any information storage and retrieval system without permission in writing from the copyright owner.

ISBN: 978-1-947829-92-3
For Worldwide Distribution
Printed in the U.S.A.

Please visit our website: diane-divine.com

Touch Point Productions & Publishing
Long Island, NY

To my family

Contents

POETRY 1
JANUARY 3
Dr. Martin Luther King 4
New Year 5
Mr. Cold 6
Snowy Days 7
Dr. King 8
Justice 9
FEBRUARY 11
Valentine's Day 12
Famous People in History 13
George Washington 14
Abraham Lincoln 15
February 16
MARCH 17
March Winds 18
Leprechauns 19
Saint Patrick's Day 20
It's Spring 21
APRIL 23
April 24
What Makes Rain? 25
Rainy Days 26
Recycle 27
MAY 29
Mothers 30
Mother's Day 31
Grandparents 32
Grandparents, We Love You 33

A Spring Holiday 34
Cinco de Mayo 35
Flowers 36
JUNE 37
June 38
Father 39
Fathers 40
Graduation Day 41
Summer 42
Our Flag 43
JULY 45
Fourth of July 46
Sunny Days 47
AUGUST 49
August 50
My Bike 51
SEPTEMBER 53
School 54
My Education 55
Fall 56
Apples 57
OCTOBER 59
Halloween 60
I'm a Little Ghost 61
Columbus 62
NOVEMBER 63
Thanksgiving 64
Veterans 65
Veteran's Day 66

DECEMBER 67
- December Holidays 68
- Winter 69
- We Celebrate Kwanza 70
- Gingerbread Cookie 71
- Signs of Winter 72
- December Holidays #2 73

MISCELLANEOUS 75
- A Map 76
- A Story 77
- American People 78
- Art 79
- As I Wait for the Bus 80
- At School 81
- Basketball 82
- Body Parts 83
- Busy Day 84
- Changes 85
- Computers 86
- Drama 87
- Equality 88
- Family 89
- First Day of School 90
- Fish 91
- Food Pyramid 92
- Forest 93
- Friendship 94
- Friendship Chain 95
- Going to the Nurse 96

Gingerbread House	97
Good Morning, Sun	98
Good Night, Moon	99
Guitar Playing Principal	100
Homework	101
I Know We Can Be Friends	102
I Like Myself	103
I Love	104
I Love to Read	105
I Want Children to Learn	106
If You Were a Teacher	107
Kindergarten Reading	108
Library	109
Life	110
Lunchroom	111
Math	112
Months of the Year	113
Music	114
Onomatopoeia	115
Pancakes/Flap Jacks	116
Pattern Book	117
Patterns, Patterns	118
Pets, Pets	119
Photosynthesis	120
Physical Education	121
Plants	122
Playground	123

Principal 124
Science 125
Seasons 126
Soccer 127
Social Studies 128
Something Has to Move You 129
The Play 130
Tired 131
Twos 132
Water 133
When You Write a Story 134

POETRY

Poetry, poetry
Words in verse
We write wonderfully
We write about
A thought we have
Then continue it
Down a poetry path.

Poetry, poetry
Short and sweet
We guarantee
We pick a topic
We really like
Then write cool verses
That are really just right.

JANUARY

Dr. Martin Luther King

Dr. Martin Luther King was a great man.
He gave many speeches around many lands.
He spoke of freedom. He spoke of truth.
He spoke to the old and to the youth.
He spoke of peace and unity.
So this world could be a better place for you and me.

Dr. King was great. Dr. King was grand.
Dr King was the man to make a stand
For the rights of our people who've been held down.
To make a stand
For our people who've been pushed around.
To make a stand
So black and white can live in unity
So this world could be a better place for you and me.

Dr. King was brave. Dr King was strong.
There were some that thought he was wrong.
He kept his faith. He kept his dream.
Dr. King was on the winning team.
We remember him in a special way.
Now he has a holiday.
Dr. King fought non-violently
So this world could be a better place for you and me.

New Year

Another year has come to an end.
We're one year older
New things will begin.
We make resolutions
To do this and that
Be a better person, be neater
Or do less chitchat.

The memories of last year
Will linger in our mind.
We'll think about them often
From time to time.

Yet we're eager to experience
New situations and tasks.
New discoveries and adventures,
New questions to ask.

This new year will be exciting
Filled with new things and old
As we progress further
To achieve our goals.

Mr. Cold

Mr. Cold, Mr. Cold
Bitter frost
Zip your coats
Mr. Cold is boss.

He wants to get into
Every unguarded place.
So button your buttons
And cover your face.

Snowy Days

Snow, snow
Beautiful snow
Falling lightly
wherever I go.

Outside when I see a winter wonderland,
I dream of being in a foreign land
Where there is lots and lots of snow
And people build snowmen wherever they go.

Dr. King

D is for DARE,

    Dr. King dared to have a dream.

R is for REMEMBER,

    We must always remember what it means.

K is for KINDNESS,

    He used kindness to conquer hate.

I is for IMPRESSIVE,

    The man was truly great.

N is for NECESSARY,

    The world needed a man so brave.

G is for GENTLE,

    He gave, and gave, and gave.

Dr. King has inspired us all,
To do our best and always stand tall.
Happy Birthday, Dr. King!

J-U-S-T-I-C-E

DR. KING STOOD FOR JUSTICE.

J is for JOYFUL, That's how the people felt.
      When Dr. King gave his speeches,
      His presence was heartfelt.
U is for UNDERSTANDING, Dr. King really was.
      When he came onto the scene,
      So fresh and so clean,
      His presence caused a buzz.
S is for SERIOUS, Dr. King was a serious man.
      He gave speeches all around.
      He had a really great plan.
T is for TRUST, He had the people's trust.
      If you want to lead anyone,
      This really is a must.
I is for IMPORTANT, Dr. King did important things.
      He helped to change a lot of terrible laws,
      And helped make freedom ring.
C is for COURAGE, It took courage to fight the good fight.
      He wanted all people to unite together.
      It shouldn't matter if you're black or white.
E is for EXCELLENT, Dr. King made a difference in this world.
      He was a man of excellence.
      He helped every man, woman, boy, and girl.

DR. KING STOOD FOR JUSTICE.

FEBRUARY

Valentine's Day

I like you.
You like me.
So please be my Valentine
and play with me.

We are friends.
We play in school.
Let's play with others too.
I think that's cool.

Valentine's Day
Valentine's Day
Sweethearts, candies,
and cards that say
Lots of things we like to hear
From friends and loved ones
we hold dear.

Famous People in History

Famous people
in history
Did great things
for the world to see.

Some were brave,
Some were strong,
Some made things right
when things were wrong.

We learn about them
at home and school.
Our teacher tells us
they were really cool.

George Washington

The very first president
we ever had.
He made good decisions
He made people glad.

He was a general
in an army during war.
He promised to do his best,
he always swore.

He was mighty in battles
and won each one he fought.
He led his men to victory
with an army he wrought.

He was a great leader
as everyone can tell.
His work speaks for itself
He served his country well.

Abraham Lincoln

Honest Abe
Honest Abe
He signed the Emancipation Proclamation,
which freed the slaves.

He wore a tall hat.
He had a black beard.
To many people,
he was very dear.

A tall, gentle man,
You would notice right away.
We commemorate his life
with a holiday.

February

Lincoln, Washington,
Valentine's Day
Winter recess
It's really okay.

African-American History Awareness
The shortest month
It's really the best.

MARCH

March Winds

March winds blow
to and fro.
Swirling, twirling,
Watch them go.

Fly a kite.
Watch it dance
to the music of the wind.
It will play and prance.

Leprechauns

Leprechaun fairies
Little and green
They live in the forest
They're usually never seen.

They have a pot of gold,
and they sneak around.
If you make a wish,
they may be found.

You can take their gold
If you're very bold
And not too old.
You may get a scold
That's what I'm told.

But that's okay
Just take it really fast
And run away.

Saint Patrick's Day

Leprechauns, shamrocks, and pots of gold
Traditions kept from days of old.
Little Irishmen in little green suits
With wide-collared shirts and buckles on boots.

Fairytales and myths, some people believe.
It's all in good fun, even if you can't conceive.
They came from Ireland with hopes that wouldn't fade.
They celebrate their heritage with a parade.

And also Saint Patrick was a special man,
A good and honest person who gave a helping hand.
Some observe this special day with family and friends
And can't wait till next year to celebrate again.

It's Spring

It's spring, it's spring
The flowers are here.
Sun and rain have helped us to grow.
This is our time
So we will shine
On this bright and wonderful day.

It's spring, it's spring
The flowers sing,
Our bright, pretty colors we show.
The time is right
Let's shine our light
until our time is done.

APRIL

April

April flowers
blooming and aglow.
April showers
helped them to grow.

April Fool's Day
I tricked you.
April fun.
Such great things to do.

What Makes Rain?

The sun heats the water on the land,
which evaporates all the water.
The water rises into the air,
in a form called vapor, which is a gas.

In time, the water vapor cools
and condenses to form tiny droplets in the clouds.
The droplets come together to form bigger drops,
which fall as rain.

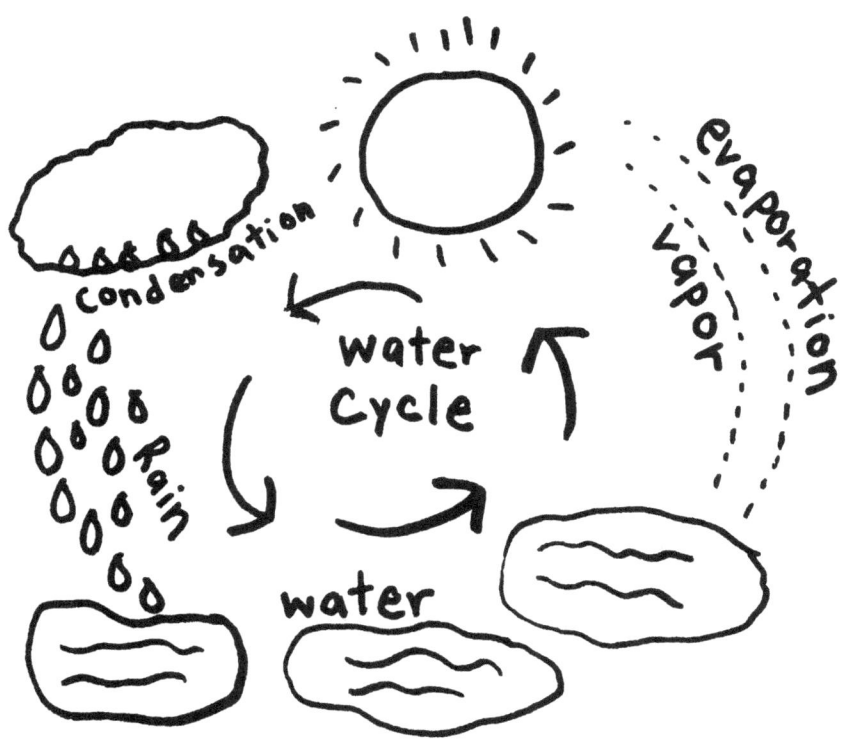

Rainy Days

Rainy days, rainy days
I get to wear my slicker.
I splash in puddles,
Stick my tongue out in the rain,
I don't get to school much quicker.

Drip, drop
Pitter, patter
I hear these sounds all day.
I try to imitate them
As I work and play.

Rain, rain
Stay a while.
I hear you for miles and miles.
Your downpour makes me smile.
I know you're just watering the earth.

Recycle

Newspapers, plastic,
bottles, and cans.
Don't put these things
in the trash can.

We can recycle
and use them again.
Put these items
in recycling bins!

MAY

Mothers

Mothers are very special
They help us all the time
They make sure we have things we need
and also nourish our minds.

They're really great to talk to
when something is bothering us.
They always know the right things to say.
In mothers, we do trust.

Mother's Day

M—is for Many.　　So many things you do.
　　　　　　　　　You help us in so many ways.
　　　　　　　　　And love us through and through.
O—is for Occasions.　You remember everyone.
　　　　　　　　　Birthdays, holidays, and special days.
　　　　　　　　　We always have lots of fun.
T—is for Terrific.　　You really, really are.
　　　　　　　　　You light up the world.
　　　　　　　　　Just like bright, shining stars.
H—is for Happy.　　You make us smile each day.
　　　　　　　　　If we are sad, you make us glad.
　　　　　　　　　You really know the right things to say.
E—is for Enormous.　An enormous responsibility you bear.
　　　　　　　　　You do so much without a fuss.
　　　　　　　　　We really know you care.
R—is for Relax.　　That's what we want you to do.
　　　　　　　　　On this, your very special day.
　　　　　　　　　Happy Mother's Day to you!

Grandparents

G—is for Great
R—is for Radiant
A—is for Accommodating
N—is for Nice
D—is for Dear
P—is for Patient
A—is for Admirable
R—is for Remarkable
E—is for Exciting
N—is for Needful
T—is for Terrific

It doesn't matter if they're near or far
S—is for Sweet
Grandparents really are!

Grandparents, We Love You

When Grandpa or Grandma come over,
We're so, so happy all day.
They're really glad to see us too
And they really have a lot to say.

We talk and talk for hours
We have a lot of fun too.
There are lots of hugs and kisses
Grandparents, we love you.

A Spring Holiday

Chocolate bunnies
Baskets with eggs
Cottontail bunnies hopping
On their hind legs.

Cute little bonnets
Dressed so nice
Treats in baskets
Filled with sugar and spice.

Bright colored eggs
Hidden behind trees
Or in flower gardens
Watch out for the bees.

Who'll find the most?
We all have so much fun.
Friends and families gather
Until the day is done.

Cinco de Mayo

Cinco de Mayo,
the fifth of May.
Mexicans remember
A battle that day.

Benito Juarez,
the Mexican president,
Helped win the war they fought
against the French.

Flowers

Flowers, flowers,
Pretty to see.
They all are plants,
Just like a tree.

They come in many colors,
shapes, and sizes.
Some have sweet scents.
They're very pleasing to the eye.

JUNE

June

June, June
big red balloons.
Carnivals, circuses
come to town soon.

School is now over.
Do enjoy the sun.
What a great time!
Summer has begun.

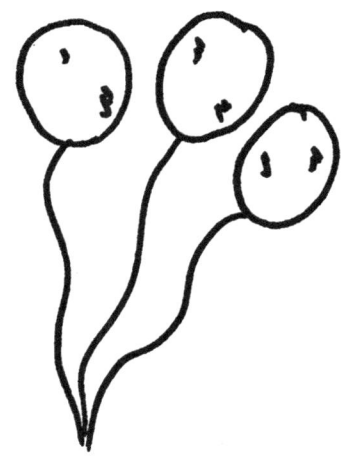

Father

F—is for Family. An important member you are.
 You make us feel real special,
 Whether you're near or far.

A—is for Always. You always think of us.
 You help us learn and make us laugh.
 You always do so much.

T—is for Togetherness. Togetherness we share.
 If you are home or at work,
 We always know you care.

H—is for Happy. We always share great times.
 You make us excited and delighted.
 Great memories we'll always find.

E—is for Enjoyment. We enjoy having you around.
 To run and play and make our day.
 You're a king who deserves a crown.

R—is for Relax. That's what we want you to do.
 On this very special day,
 Happy Father's Day to you!

Fathers

Fathers, fathers
Fathers are brave and strong.
Children and fathers
We really get along.

Some fathers work so long and hard
They're not always home all the time.
But that's okay
They love us more each day
And everything is just fine.

Graduation Day

We woke up early this morning,
Had breakfast and got dressed.
We knew it was a special day,
So we really look our best.

We're leaving kindergarten.
We worked hard all year through.
Today is graduation day!
We'll share this day with you.

We're going to first grade now.
Don't worry, we'll be fine.
We'll say good-bye.
Now don't you cry.
Great memories stay in our mind.

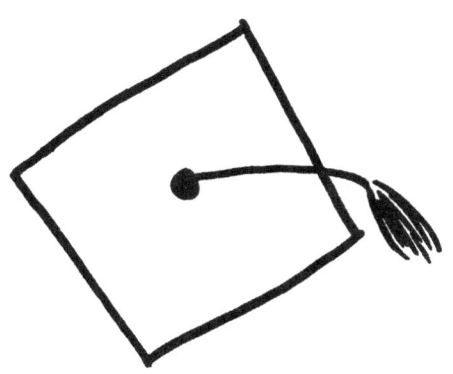

Summer

Camps, vacations
Summer sun.
Outings, trips
And summer fun.

Parties, functions
Summer madness.
When summer's over
Summer sadness.

Our Flag

An American symbol,
It stands for our nation's pride.
We display the flag at half staff
When an important person has died.

Our flag has fifty stars
for all the United States.
Thirteen stripes for the colonies
Our flag is really great.

To me it stands for safety
A protected nation are we.
To me it stands for celebration
For we all have liberty.

White stands for purity
Red stands for bravery
Blue stands for justice
We have the victory!

Wave your flag in victory.
We are the land of the free!
Wave your flag in victory.
We are the land of the free!

JULY

Fourth of July

A sparkling holiday
Marching in parades
Many bands are playing
It's Independence Day.

Fire engines rolling
Police are marching too.
Many schools are represented
There are so many things to do.

At night there is a light show
With many fireworks
Done by professional workers
So no one will get hurt.

Pop, pop, popping
Firecrackers light up the sky.
This happens every year
On the Fourth of July.

Sunny Days

Sunny days
They're the best
I get to wear
my pretty dress.

Or shorts and t-shirt
Sandals without socks.
I'll go to the park
Play in the sandbox.

Or go to the beach
with my bathing suit on
Splash in the water
Sing a few songs.

Then eat my lunch
as I lie on the sand.
And I won't forget the sunscreen
to rub on my legs, arms, and hands.

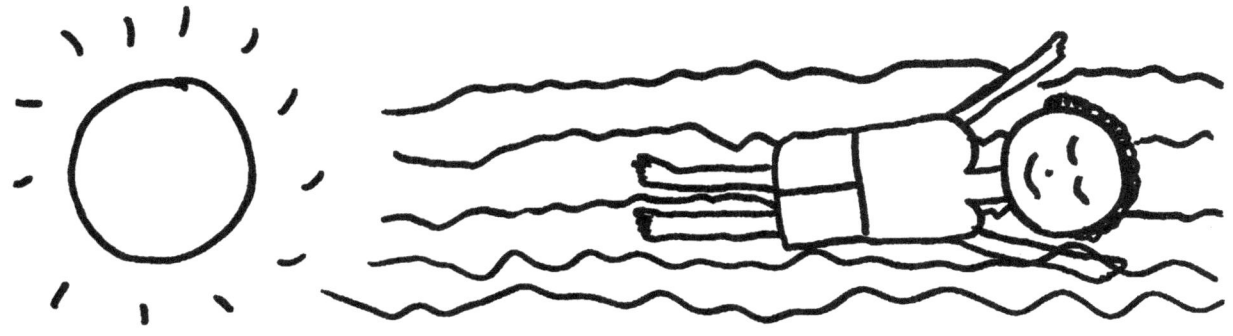

AUGUST

August

No special holidays
or things to do.
Just regular summer days
and things to get into.

Such as summer trips
The weather should be great
Cycling or tennis
Or going to the park on skates.

Loving every minute
of every wonderful day
Celebrating life
No matter come what may.

My Bike

I like to ride my shiny bike
up and down my block.
My mom says, "Don't forget your helmet."
In the summer, I ride a lot.

I just ride on the sidewalk now
or maybe I'll go to the park.
I always follow rules
and never try to be cool,
and I never ride after dark.

SEPTEMBER

School

September, September. School begins.
We bought all our supplies and a few extra pens.
Our radiant faces show excitement within
As well as curiosity of our newfound friends.

Who will they be? What will they be like?
Will we get along? Oh, I hope we don't fight.
And how about our teacher? I hope she is great.
I hope we get along well, not someone I grow to hate.

But I've made a vow to be good in school.
Do all of my work and follow the rules.
Oh, I may slip up, as children sometimes do.
But I'll get right back on track and continue to pursue.

I'll have a great school year,
I really do believe.
I'll learn a lot this year
And achieve, achieve, achieve.

My Education

For my education
I know that it's best
To attend all classes
With no foolishness.

To listen carefully
And adhere to all the rules.
Won't be so concerned
With acting real cool.

I'll just be myself,
Completing all my work.
Helping others when I can,
Not acting like a jerk.

Not provoking others
To become annoyed with me.
Instead, I'll strive real hard
And be the very best I can be.

Fall

Yellow, orange
Red and brown
Colorful leaves
Are flying around.

Winds blow softly
Fast and slow.
Swirling, swirling,
Watch them go.

Apples

First, you plant an apple seed,
Then you give it what it needs:
Water, air, and heat from the sun,
Then apple buds bloom, one by one.

Pollination must happen
for the tree to bear fruit.
So many glorious blossoms
They really look so cute.

So, they're visited by bees
who do their job as well.
They move into the orchids
And there, they dwell.

Until it's time to leave
Then flower petals fall.
They bring joy to us all.

Red, yellow, green
and mixtures too.
I really love apples.
How about you?

OCTOBER

Halloween

Maybe I'll be a ghost
Maybe I'll be a queen
Maybe I'll be a fireman
On this Halloween.

I'll paint my face with make-up
Maybe my mom will help
She can make or buy the costume
I'll put it on myself.

We'll march around in our costumes
And have a great parade
And then we'll have a party
With treats and lemonade.

Then we'll go trick-or-treating
To familiar homes nearby
With parents, sisters, brothers, and friends,
We'll have a wonderful time.

I'm a Little Ghost

I'm a little ghost,
scary and white.
I fly through the air
in the dark, dark night.

When it's Halloween time,
I fly in sight.
And scare boys and girls.
Oh, what a fright!

Columbus

He sailed across the ocean
With three quite remarkable ships.
The queen gave him the money
So he was properly equipped.

Many people believed the earth
was very, very flat
And that Columbus would fall off the world
And never, ever come back.

But Columbus proved them wrong
He sailed to great lands too.
Places he had never seen
To Columbus, they were new.

He saw red-faced people
who were Native Americans.
Columbus named these people.
He called them Indians.

He brought back evidence of his findings.
People were very impressed.
He became a famous man
He did his very best.

NOVEMBER

Thanksgiving

The Pilgrims came to America
A long, long time ago.
They came from a place called England
They didn't like it there, so...

They came seeking new freedom
And a new way of life.
But after they sailed to America
They had many troubles and strife.

The Native Americans were helpful.
They showed them many things
Like how to build houses, plant crops, and hunt
And survive through the trials life brings.

Then one day they came together
All dressed in traditional clothes.
They shared a big feast together
Well, you know how the story goes.

This feast was a way of saying thank you,
Sharing together with family and friends.
There were smiles and good feelings all around
And that's the way Thanksgiving has always been.

Veterans

Veterans are really special
They really, really are.
They have helped protect our country
From enemies near and far.

Army, Navy, Coast Guard, Marines,
And the Air Force too.
Make up the five Armed Service Branches.
Each of them is tried and true.

Men and women working together
To achieve some common goals,
Which are peace, security, protection, and help
For our country as a whole.

So, today we truly salute you
For the thorough work you've done.
Your courage through hard times,
Your bravery will not be undone.
Each of you are Number One!

Veteran's Day

We remember the soldiers
Who served our country well.
From the past to the present,
Oh the stories they could tell.

We set aside this day,
To remember them in our hearts.
In the history of our nation,
They will always be a part.

DECEMBER

December Holidays

December holidays are really nice,
They're extra special and filled with spice.
They're a time for giving and sharing great times
With family and friends who are so, so kind.

Relatives come to visit
We haven't seen in a while.
Some come from distant places
They travel miles and miles.

We share precious memories
And remember old times,
We gather at the table,
Say grace, and dine.

We play games together,
We open gifts and toys.
There's love all around us.
The days are filled with joy.

Winter

Cold, cold weather
Everywhere we go.
We have to wear our coats and scarves
No more grass to mow

Red, red noses
All around
Cold fingers and snow
No more flowers grow

Temperatures inside are high
Temperatures outside are low.
And don't forget
Mr. Ho, Ho, Ho.

We Celebrate Kwanza

We celebrate Kwanza
We celebrate today.
We celebrate Kwanza
in a very special way.

Kwanza is a holiday
We share with family and friends.
We honor African traditions
Seven principles we extend.

Kwanza is a celebration
of the future, present, and past.
We light the Kwanza candles,
Seven days it will last.

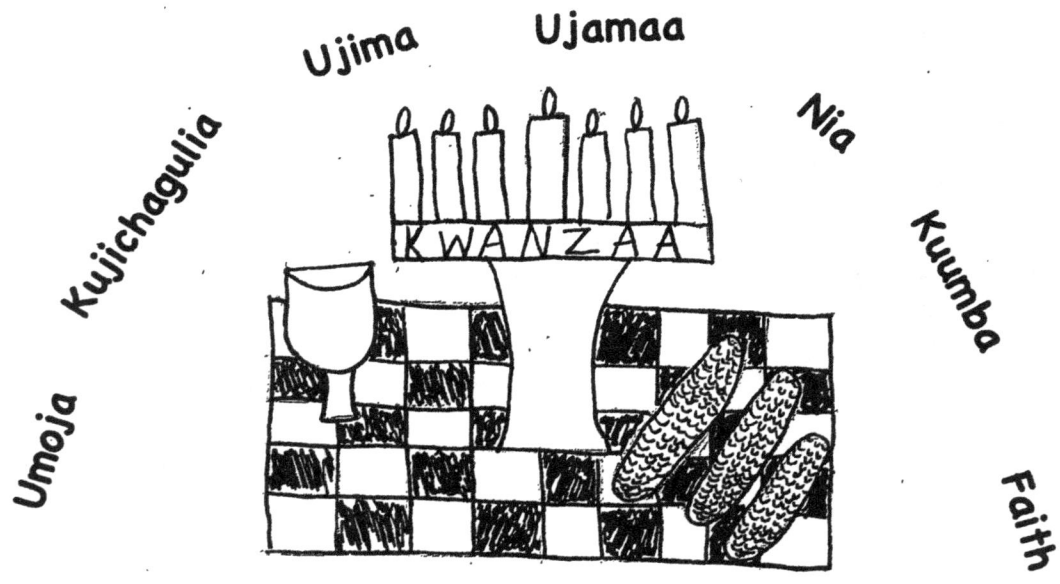

Gingerbread Cookie

Gingerbread cookies are great to taste.
In stories they run away in haste.
But that's really not true.
I've eaten quite a few.
And when I get one,
I'll say thank you!

Signs of Winter

Signs of winter
Begin to show.
Weather gets colder,
Winds blow and blow.

December holidays
Are in full bloom.
January and February
go by soon.

We build snowmen in the snow.
I see a winter wonderland all aglow.
Dr. Martin Luther King, George Washington,
And Abraham Lincoln too.

Are important winter birthdays
Just to name a few.
Winter holds many wonderful things.
But before you know it,
Here comes spring!

December Holidays #2

Merry Christmas!
Happy Hanukkah!
Happy Kwanza too!
These are December holidays
We'll celebrate with you.

Light the Menorah!
Light the Kinara!
Decorate the Christmas tree!
Everyone celebrates something,
Including you and me.

MISCELLANEOUS

A Map

Drawings of the earth's surface
Countries, cities, seas
Drawings of roads, streets, and buildings
We can add fields and trees.

Lines and shapes show details
Arranged in such an array.
North, South, East, West,
These directions help show us the way.

A map is a very useful tool
It's very important to us.
It helps us get to where we have to go
You can use a map key as a plus.
Google Maps really does it for us.

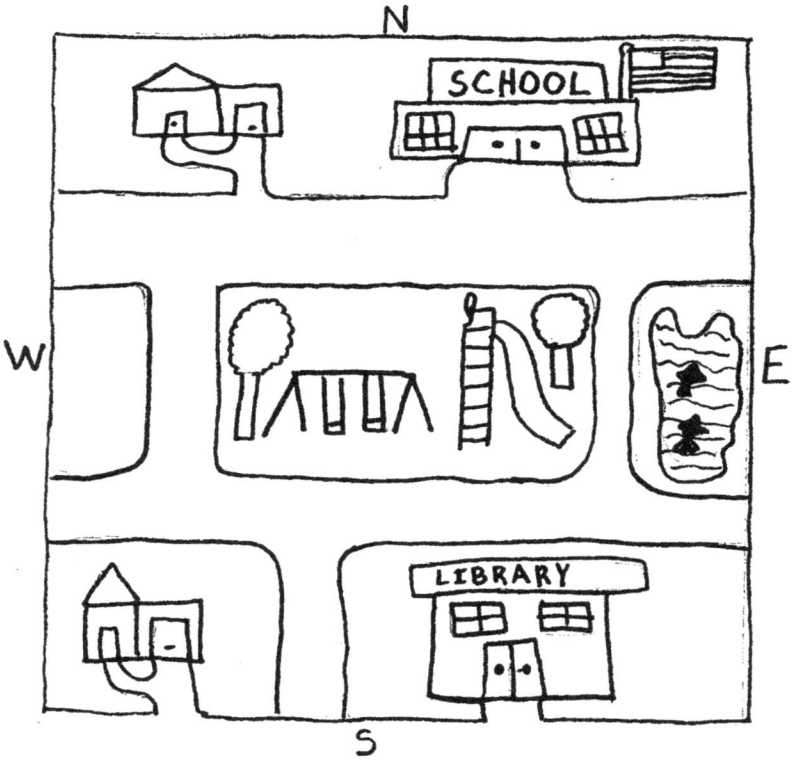

A Story

Today I'll write a story.
Now let me get my supplies.
First, I'll need some paper.
I must get just the right size.

Next, I'll need my markers.
I'll get every single one.
I might not even use them all,
But, boy, will I have fun!

Now, I'll be creative.
I'll write exactly what I want to say.
I'll use inventive spelling
I'll do everything my way.

I'll put it all together and staple it.
Finally I'm done.
I'll read to my teacher and friends
A story I wrote just for fun.

American People

We learn about American people,
important people,
who've made a difference in our world.
They each had a goal.
Young minds, they help mold.
So we'll remember them
and not let their spirit die.

We learn about American people,
important people,
who've paved the way
for many of us today.
We salute them all in time,
very earnestly.
And they're all part of our history.

Art

Painting, drawing,
Cutting out.
Doing my best
without a doubt.

Staying inside the line
Not using too much glue
Sharing materials
Doing what I have to do.

Being creative,
Expressing myself well,
Being an artist
My work is just swell.

As I Wait for the Bus

I saw a ladybug,
Crawling up a tree.
My mommy held my hand,
While she waited with me.

It started to drizzle a little.
We forgot the umbrella, oh no!
I guess I'll just put on my hood
I hope it doesn't start to snow.

The wind is blowing harder.
When will the bus finally come?
All I know is this waiting
Is really not much fun.

At School

I can run. I can play.
I can write and work all day.
I can sing. I can act.
I can eat my lunch, and I can snack.

I can learn and follow rules.
I can be myself at school.
I can dance. I can rest.
I can sit nicely at my desk.

Basketball

Swoosh! Swoosh!
Jammin' in the basket.
Sweet lay-ups with a delicate touch.
It feels like I'm floating on air.

Oh, you had the ball
Now I do
Another steal
Now, let me see
What should I do?

Should I pass it to someone
Or dribble it up myself?
Maybe a combination of both
I don't want to be selfish.

A team works together
The ultimate result
Should be based on teamwork.

Body Parts

We have one head
Under that we have a neck.
Two shoulders and two arms
Our chest and stomach connect.

Then comes our lower body,
Our legs follow next.
Our feet are on the bottom,
And we know all the rest!

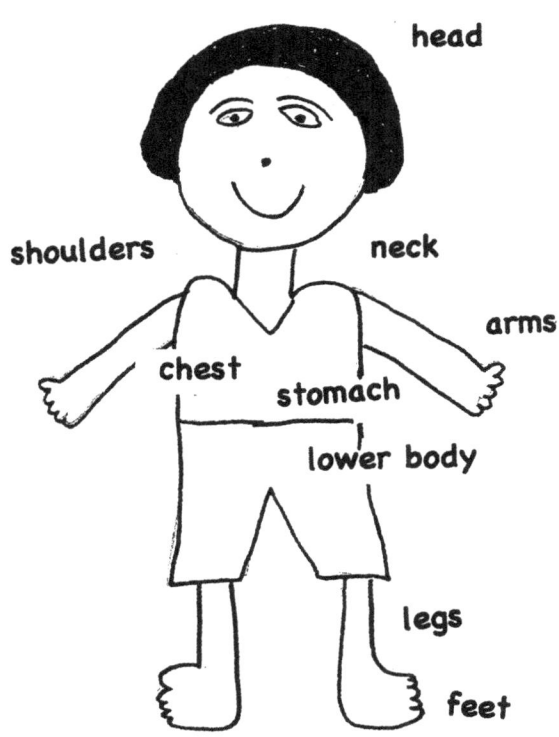

Busy Day

Today we had a busy day.
We did so much in school.
We heard and read a story.
We did a story map,
Went to centers and followed rules.

After lunch and recess,
We had five minutes of quiet time.
Then it was time to go to our special.
So we all got back on line.

Afterwards, we played a math game.
Then we did a follow-up sheet.
I wrote and illustrated a story,
Which made my day complete.

I can't wait until tomorrow
To learn a new poem or song,
To do something new,
With a friend or two.
Oh, how well we get along.

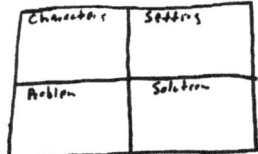

Changes

Changes, changes
One, two, three.
Everything must change, you see.

First we're young
Then we grow older.
The weather gets warm,
Then it gets colder.

Changes, changes
One, two, three.
The world around us changes, you see.

Plants and animals
People and places
They all change.

Computers

I can turn the computer on,
all by myself.
I can log in and work on programs
with very little help.

I can draw a picture
and print it with ease.
I'll write a story too.
Computers are a breeze.

Drama

Turn it on
Let it loose.
Work it out
Let it move you.

Experience it
Get into it
Be it
Love it
Drama.

Equality

E is for Everyone here
    so listen up and open up your ears.
Q is for Qualify, we all do
    so let's give it a try.
U is for Unity, united we stand
    that's the way it should be.
A is for Abolishment, take away the hatred
    let's make an attempt.
L is for the Love in our hearts, caring for others
    that's a great start.
I is for Improvement in life, accepting everyone
    red, yellow, brown, black, or white.
T is for Togetherness, divided we fall
    let's not be selfish.
Y is for the Young and the Old, working as one
    to achieve the same goal.

Every person is different and special in their own way.
Let's be fair to everyone and not judge them, come what may.
The uniqueness of all is cultural to see
So always strive for EQUALITY.

Family

F is for Feelings we share each day
    with many family members in different ways.
A is for Always, we'll always be together
    caring and sharing, through all kinds of weather.
M is for Merry, we're happy as can be
    We love everybody, especially family.
I is for Important, all families really are
    no matter where they live.
    They could be near or far.
L is for Love, they show to us always
    at many different times, in many different ways.
Y is for Yes, we really do agree
    that families are a precious gift
    everyone can see.

        Families are special
        They're great to be around
        They'll bring your spirits up
        If you are feeling down.

        They're really unique people
        With many styles and ways.
        We love to be around them
        We love our Family Days.

First Day of School

I know there's something I'm missing.
There's something I forgot to do.
I made all the names
And prepared special games.
Yellow balloons on a stick I blew.

I spoke with all the parents.
I assured them this day would go fine.
All the excited faces,
Maybe a few shoe unlaces.
I made great plans to fill up the time.

The excitement is growing and growing.
I knew this day would come.
And now it's finally here.
Let's give a cheer.
We'll put a smile on that face that looks glum.

Hopefully by the end of the day.

Fish

Swim little fish
A bigger fish wants lunch.
He's coming after you.
Munch, munch, munch.

There will always be danger
Fish will come, and they will go.
In this big, beautiful ocean,
Some move fast, and some move slow.

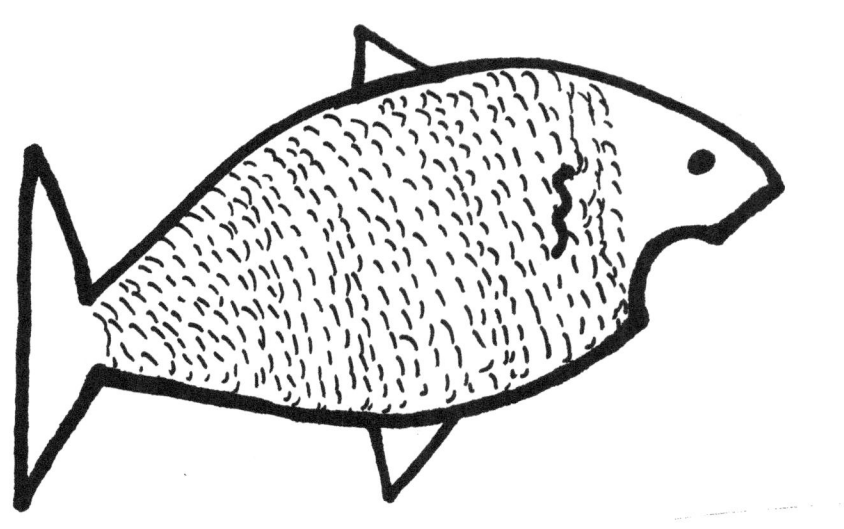

Food Pyramid

Meat and proteins
Bread and grains
Fruits and vegetable
for our body and brain.

Milk and dairy products
We should eat as a kid.
And less extra foods
From the food pyramid.

Forest

Tigers, grizzlies, orangutans.
Little crawly bugs
in the pond and on land.

Snakes are slithering,
Birds are at their best.
These are some of the amazing sights
in the great forest.

Friendship

What do you like to do?
Oh, I like that too.
Maybe we can do it together
Just me and you.

If Sheena wants to play,
She can come along.
We can all play together
Maybe we'll sing some songs.

Or show each other dances
We learned from some cartoon
Try to do this move
Oh, that was really smooth.

Or maybe draw a picture
of a beautiful summer day.
We can all share my crayons
Just don't break them, okay?

Friendship Chain

I made a special friendship chain.
I made it nice and long.
All my friends have added a link
It stands for friendships strong.

It symbolizes kindness,
Encouragement and caring too.
It also stands for togetherness,
And friendships tried and true.

The friendship chain reminds me,
In love and respect we should abound.
Be courteous and kind all the time.
Good friends won't let you down.

Going to the Nurse

Oh, I cut my finger.
My boo boo really hurts.
I know it's just a paper cut.
I'll have to go to the nurse.

She'll make it feel better.
She'll dry my tears and all.
Now I can go back to the room,
But not running in the halls.

Gingerbread House

Gingerbread house.
Gingerbread house.
Decorated with candy,
lots of treats,
sour and sweet.
Boy, that's really dandy.

Come inside.
Come inside.
Come inside and join us.
We're so happy to see you
inside our gingerbread house.

Good Morning, Sun

Good morning, sun
The day has begun.
There's lots of things to do.
Put on some clothes
Because who knows
The situations we'll get into.

Let's do some work
Don't be a jerk.
Let's use our minds to think.
And keep in mind
We don't have much time
We'd rather float than sink.

Good Night, Moon

Good night, moon
You came too soon
I had so much more to do.
But that's okay
I'll start the next day
Very busy all day through.

When it was night
I held my pillow tight,
Hoping the night wouldn't last long.
I had to count sheep
In order to get to sleep
I couldn't wait to get up
And sing my song.

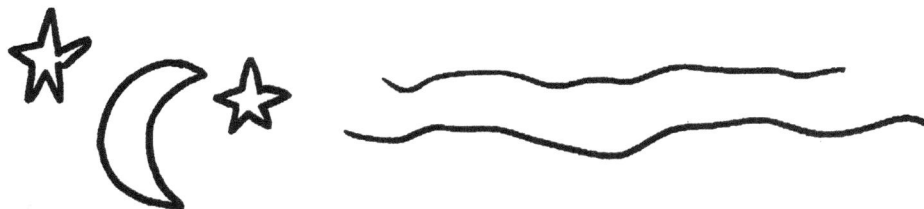

Guitar Playing Principal
(Ode to Mr. Newman)

Guitar playing principal,
Play a song for me.
You know all the Beatle's songs
Why don't you play "Let It Be"?

As you walk through the halls
or make phone calls,
School business you oversee.
Whenever you get a little break,
why don't you play a song for me?

Guitar playing principal
in school at the crack of dawn.
You work so hard and diligently
You're in school till the last student has gone.

On your feet all day,
getting things underway.
But when the day gets worry-free,
and you get finished with all your administrative duties,
why don't you play a song for me?

Homework

I know the teacher explained it.
We did this work in school.
I'm almost sure I know it,
But now it seems I'm running out of fuel.

I better take my notes out
And review what we did in class today.
Maybe I'll call my friend also,
Maybe she can help in some way.

Wait! I feel my second wind coming.
I'm finally starting to understand.
My temporary memory block is gone.
Now I'm back in command.

Temporary memory loss comes and goes.
I'm glad mine came back in time.
So I could do what I needed to do.
Now I have peace of mind.

I Know We Can Be Friends

Let's be kind
All the time
Helping friends
A smile is a sign.
Let's shake hands
I know we can be friends
Let's encourage
Friends every day.
Helping others
Makes my day.
Let's shake hands
I know we can be friends.

I Like Myself

I like myself
I like my smile
I like my clothes
I like my style.

I like the way I dance
and play basketball.
I like myself
when I shop at the mall.

I like when I help others
when they need a helping hand.
I like when I assist
and think of a plan.

I like myself
and this is true.
But I also like my friends
and playing with you!

I Love...

I love pumpkins
I love fish
I love my family
I love to make a wish.

I love sunny days
and playing outside.
I love skateboards
and bikes to ride.

I love parties
and a shopping spree.
I love school
and I love me!

I Love to Read

What subject do I want?
What book shall I pick?
Shall I choose something funny
or a drama with a little kick?

Shall I choose non-fiction or fiction?
What am I in the mood for?
Maybe I'll read a biography
and learn more and more
about a particular person.

I'll let my heart take the lead.
There are so many topics to choose from.
Oh my, do I love to read!

I Want Children to Learn

I want children to learn
something new every day.
Embrace each moment
of creative work and play.

I want children to learn
to think highly of themselves.
Have confidence within
to have success again and again.

I want children to learn
all failures aren't bad.
Maybe it's just a wake-up call
to straighten up a tad.

I want children to learn
and discover something new every day.
To continuously expand their horizons
to help map out their way.

If You Were a Teacher

If you were a teacher
with a classroom next to mine,
We'd share great thoughts and ideas
and really have great times.

We'd plan for all the holidays,
special occasions would be the best.
We'd have great food and fun
with family members invited as guests.

We'd plan interesting lessons together,
empowering students to become involved,
Stimulating their young minds,
giving them real problems to solve.

Constantly giving them guidance,
monitoring the work they do,
Giving help when needed,
and encouragement to see a task through.

So if you were a teacher
with a classroom next to mine,
I know we'd work well together,
exciting tasks we'd always find.

Kindergarten Reading

Today is my turn to read.
I brought in a special book.
I can read most of the words.
Sometimes I don't even have to look.

But my teacher says that's okay
As long as I can use picture clues
to tell about the gist of the story.
To tell, When? Why? Where? What? or Who?

I just can't wait till she calls me.
I'm really excited inside.
I know what to say.
Everything's okay.
I'll use the pictures as my guide.

Library

As I walk in
I see books all around
I go to a particular section
where books I like are found.

I slowly turn the pages,
browsing through words and pictures inside.
There are so many books to choose from,
The section is very wide.

So I narrow it down to my favorite seven.
Next week, I'll come back again.
I can't wait to get home
I won't even answer the phone
Then my reading time will begin.

Life

When life throws you a curve
and you're feeling less than great,
You want to sing your song
but instead you hesitate.

When the road ahead seems rocky
and your feet are really sore,
You want to keep on walking
but then you ask, "What for?"

When boredom starts to sink in
like a sponge absorbing water,
You better squeeze it out
before you scream and shout.

A curve ball isn't so bad
maybe you'll hit the next,
You just can't stop swinging
if you don't get what you expect.

If your sore feet are aching,
sit down and rest a while.
Don't forget your original task,
just bear it with a smile.

Boredom is only in your mind
so think busy thoughts instead.
Get up and make something happen
before you go to bed.

Lunchroom

What shall I have today?
I really feel like a change.
I always have the pizza
And it always tastes the same.

Maybe I'll try the special of the day.
I'm really in the mood for a surprise.
I hope it's okay,
and I can finish the day
without regret and asking myself why.

If I'm still hungry,
I'll just have some pie.

Math

Numbers, counting
minus, plus,
Figuring out answers
without a fuss.

Multiplication and division
sometimes get tricky.
But I remember what my teacher said
So I won't do them carelessly.

Algebra, Geometry, Calculus II
These are all the topics I can't wait to do.

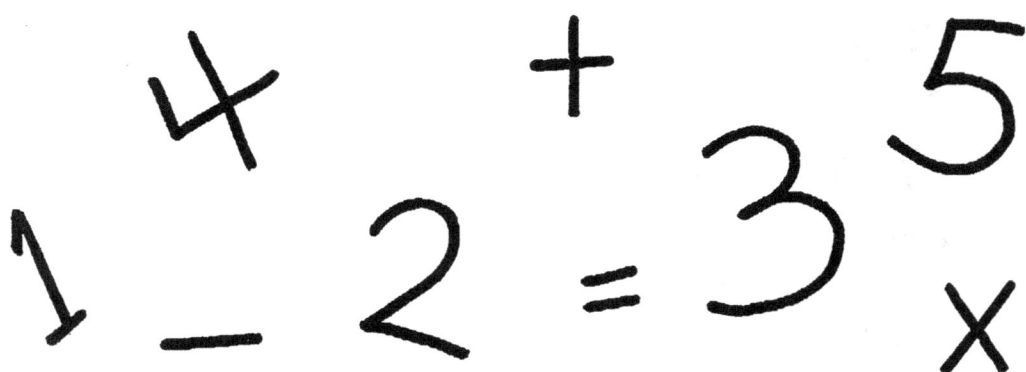

Months of the Year

Months of the year
Months of the year
Listen as we say the months of the year.

January	New Year's Day
February	Black History Month and Valentine's Day
March	Comes in like a lion
April	Spring's in the air
May	Flowers bloom
June	School's out soon
July	Independence Day
August	School's one month away
September	Hurray for school
October	Halloween is cool
November	Thanksgiving Day
December	Hanukkah, Kwanza, and Christmas Day

And then it starts over again and again
When the new year comes to an end.

Music

Singing, singing
Songs I love to sing.
The teacher plays the music
She know the words to everything.

And then she teaches us
She shows us hand movements too.
Sometimes we're up or down
She tells us what to do.

We match notes from the piano
She says we sometimes sing on key.
She's very proud of us.
I'm very proud of me.

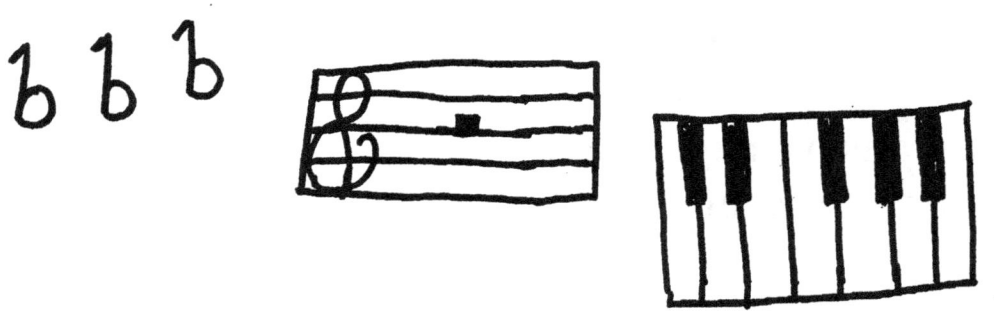

Onomatopoeia

Onamatopoeia is a long, long word.
It's a word that demonstrates
Sounds I've heard.
Such as gurgle, cluck,
Slurp and meow,
Moo, oink,
Drip drop and bow wow.

moo *munch* *quack* *slurp* *tick tock* *drip drop*

Pancakes/Flap Jacks

First you take the bowl
big and round,
Then you add the ingredients
and stir it around.

When the batter is ready,
then you heat the oil
in a big, big skillet,
But don't let it boil.

When the oil is ready
then you spoon the batter in.
You make round circles
again and again.

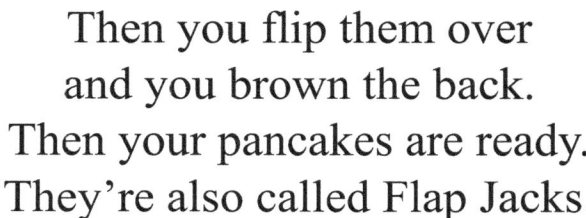

Then you flip them over
and you brown the back.
Then your pancakes are ready.
They're also called Flap Jacks.

Pattern Book

Patterns, patterns in a book
Repeated phrases, take a look.
Words we say
Again and again,
Helps young kids learn
From beginning to end.
We can make a pattern book
Open up and take a look.
Pattern books are fun,
Learning has just begun.

Patterns, Patterns

Patterns, patterns everywhere
Circle, rectangle
Triangle, and square.

Colorful designs
Wonderful to see
AB
AAB
ABC

I can make some
So can you.
Making patterns is fun to do!

△ ○ △ ○ △ ○
△ △ ○ △ △ ○
△ ○ □ △ ○ □

{ – { – { –
{ { – { { –
{ – \ { – \

Pets, Pets

Pets, pets
They're great to have.
You must take good care of them
And give them a bath.
Play and cuddle
Hug and huddle
Unless you have a pet spider.

Photosynthesis

When the light shines on
the green, green leaves
of any kind of plant,
The leaves absorb
or soak up the energy
that comes from the light.

The water and the air
inside the leaves
turn into nutrients and food.
You may not believe this,
but it's true!
It's call photosynthesis.

Physical Education

I get to wear my sneakers
and run around to play.
Of course, in an organized fashion
in a very skilled kind of way.

We do fun tasks together,
wiggling our bodies around.
Sometimes moving left or right
or jumping up and down.

It's really such a fun class
I enjoy it every time.
It's one of the best subjects
and gives me a chance to unwind.

Plants

We see plants everywhere.
Plants need water, sun, and air.
Plants are really great to have around.
We will put some in the ground.

Flowers, seeds, leaves, roots, and stem
The parts of a plant
We know all of them.
Plants come from seeds
We put in the ground.
Plants are great to have around.

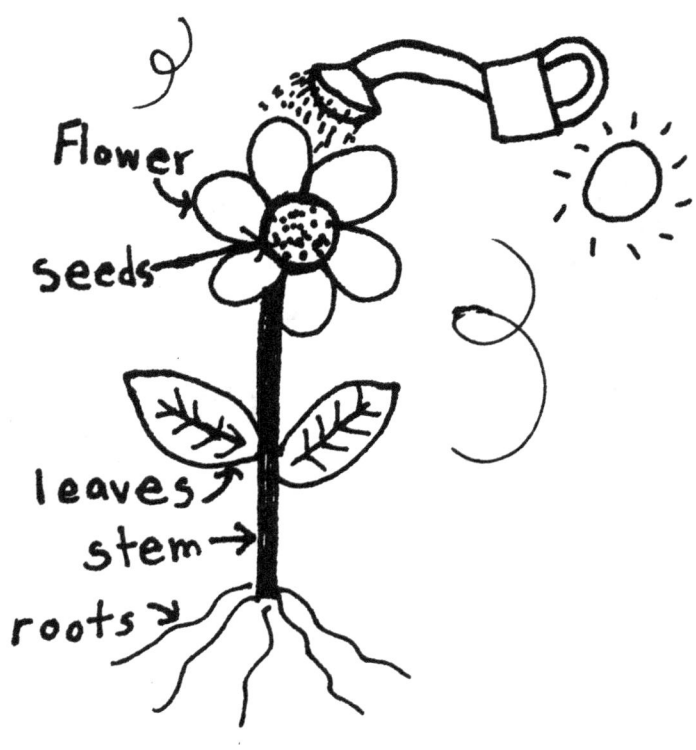

Playground

Hanging on the monkey bars,
Sliding down the slide,
Playing games together
You go seek, I'll hide.

Playing tag together
I tagged you, you're it.
Running round and round
On the school playground.

Principal

We have the greatest principal.
He's peaceful, pleasant, and polite.
He really loves frogs,
not cats or dogs.
He stands about 5'9" in height.

He's really easy to talk to
if you can steal his time.
He's a busy man,
always in demand.
He's not always easy to find.

He doesn't even have a real office.
I find this to be very rare.
The office he had
is now a computer lab.
For the students, he really cares.

So, if you ever have a problem.
He's the one you'll have to see.
He knows every child by name.
He treats them all the same
with respect and dignity.

Science

Science explorations,
Discovery, and surprise
Hypothesis proven right or wrong
Make my curiosity rise.

Putting it all together
Charting and graphing results
The data we collect
That moment to reflect
Such a great accomplishment!

Seasons

Winter, spring, summer, and fall
Are the seasons of the year.
They each show different signs
As wonderful changes appear.

In winter,
Snow is falling
It's really cold outside.

In spring,
The buds starts growing
As birds and bees arrive.

In summer,
Flowers bloom
It's really hot outside.

In fall,
Leaves are falling,
They swirl and twirl and glide.

So now we know the seasons,
Winter, spring, summer and fall.
Wonderful changes let us know
When a new season will call.

Soccer

Soccer teams competing
Guard the goalie well.
Who will win this time?
It's really hard to tell.

But it really doesn't matter
As long as you play fair
As long as you had fun
As long as you're aware:

That winning isn't everything.

Social Studies

Learning about various people
in near and faraway places,
Exciting and important events,
An array of different faces,

Some people we know
or at least heard about before.
Some unfamiliar traditions and cultures,
we'll explore.

The past, present, and future
are investigated, probed, and reviewed.
Social Studies is the subject
where we'll discover both the old and the new.

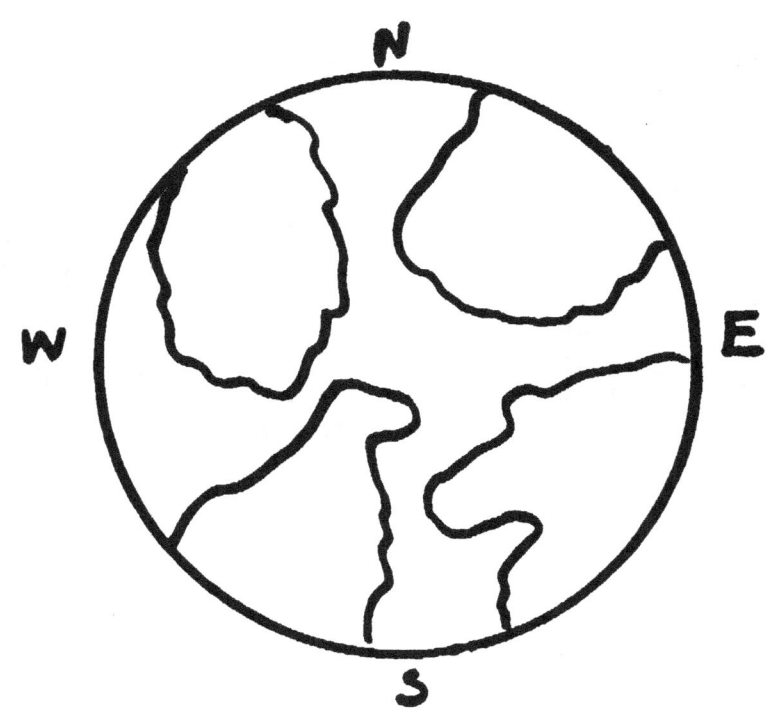

Something Has to Move You

Something has to move you
and get you excited inside.
Something has to make you tick
and make your eyes open wide.

Something has to strike you
as a really wonderful thing.
Something has to be so great
that it could make you sing.

Whatever that special something is,
just let it hit the spot.
Cherish it forever.
It may lead to an ultimate jackpot.

The Play

We're going on the stage
to perform a wonderful play.
Our teacher tells us we'll be great.
I hope I don't forget what to say.

We've been practicing our lines daily.
We really know them by heart.
We know the song
We know the moves.
Everyone knows each other's parts.

So now I guess we're ready.
Our family and friends will cheer.
Our costumes are on.
We'll keep on going if something goes wrong.
And we'll definitely have no fear.

Tired

Oh, I'm so tired.
I stayed up late last night.
I had a dance practice,
went to a game,
then we went for a bite.

I didn't even watch television.
When I got home, I read a book.
I read and read,
then I got ready for bed.
I hope there's nothing I overlooked.

I'll try to get a good sleep.
I'll wake up with a smile on my face.
I'll eat a good breakfast.
I'll say a little prayer
and try a little to ease my social pace.

Twos

Socks and gloves
Pillows and shoes
Pedals on a bike.
They all come in twos.

Ears and eyes
Arms and feet
Two by two.
They meet and greet.

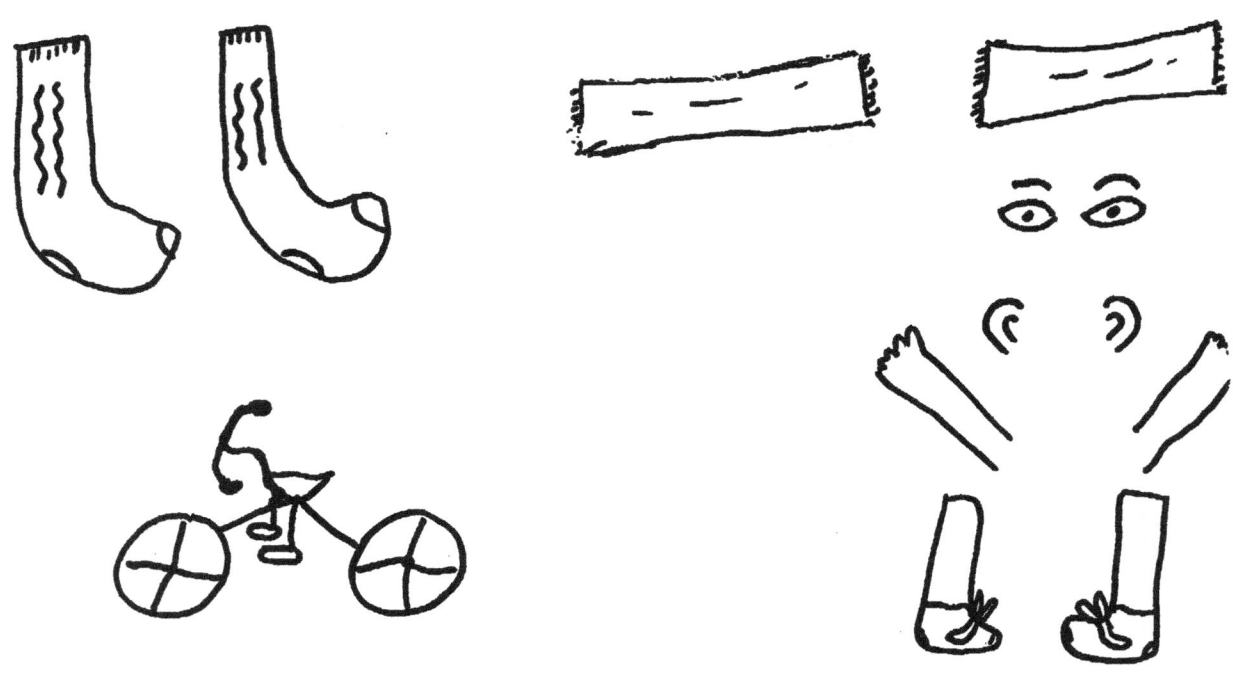

Water

Liquid, solid, gas
Liquid, solid, gas
That's what water is
That's what water is

Liquid is the water I drink.
Solid is the ice in a rink.
Gas is the steam and the vapor that shrinks

Liquid, solid, gas
Liquid, solid, gas.

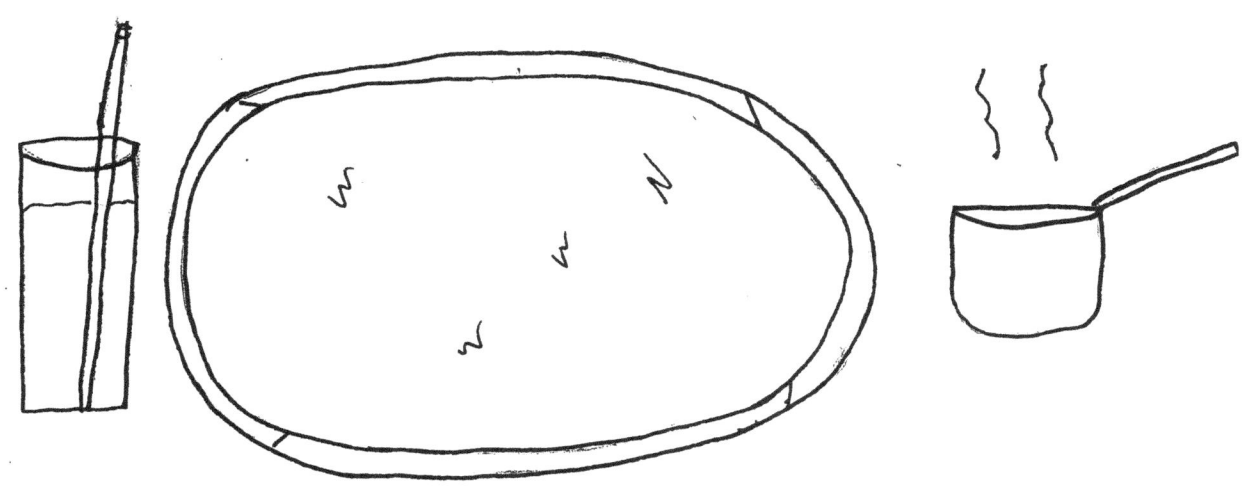

When You Write a Story

When you write a story,
This is what you do.
You think of great ideas
That are interesting too.

You start with a beginning
Then a middle
And then the end.

Don't forget to write so neat.
Don't forget to sound out words.
Don't forget to finger-space.
Don't forget the period.

Don't forget to add some parts
that tell us more.

About the Author

 Linda Taylor has molded kids' lives as a teacher for more than 25 years. She uses her poetry, songs, and chants in her kindergarten classroom to enhance learning and motivate her students. Linda holds an M.S. degree in Education from C.U.N.Y. at City College. She's the author of the Amazing Annabelle series, which has eleven chapter books and also the Daring David series with eleven chapter books. She lives in Long Island with her family.

She has also authored three other poetry books:

ALPHABET, NUMBER, AND COLOR POETRY

REALLY COOL ANIMAL POEMS

POETRY RHYMES FOR THE HEART, SOUL, AND MIND